ECLIPSE CHASER

Shadia Habbal

ECLIPSE CHASER

Science in the Moon's Shadow

by **ILIMA LOOMIS**
with photographs by **AMANDA COWAN**

Houghton Mifflin Harcourt
Boston   New York

For Lehua Katherine Salomon —IL
For Tim Dunn —AC

Library of Congress Cataloging-in-Publication Data

Names: Loomis, Ilima, author. | Cowan, Amanda (Photographer),
illustrator.
Title: Eclipse chaser : science in the moon's shadow / by Ilima Loomis ;
with photographs by Amanda Cowan.
Description: Boston ; New York : Houghton Mifflin Harcourt, [2019]
| Series: Scientists in the field | Audience: Ages 10–12. | Audience:
Grades 4 to 6.
Identifiers: LCCN 2019000890 (print) | LCCN 2019003234 (ebook) |
ISBN 9781328770967 (hardcover) | ISBN 9780358164388 (ebook)
Subjects: LCSH: Habbal, Shadia Rifai—Juvenile literature. | Total solar
eclipses—United States—Juvenile literature. | Solar eclipses—Juvenile
literature. | Astrophysicists—Juvenile literature.
Classification: LCC QB460.72.H327 (ebook) | LCC QB460.72.H327 L66
2019 (print) | DDC 523.7/8—dc23
LC record available at https://lccn.loc.gov/2019000890

Manufactured in Malaysia
TWP 10 9 8 7 6 5 4 3 2 1
4500773277

Peter Aniol uses the first stars of the night to align his telescopes.

TABLE OF CONTENTS

The total solar eclipse over Svalbard in the Arctic Circle on March 20, 2015.

MOMENT OF TRUTH

Shadia supervises as her team's luggage and equipment are loaded onto a boat in Indonesia.

S HADIA HABBAL ALMOST CAN'T BEAR to look at the sky. It's March 9, 2016, and she and her team of scientists have lugged some forty cases of equipment halfway across the world to Plun Island, Indonesia. They are here to observe a total solar eclipse. When she stepped outside her bungalow at four o'clock this morning to check the sky, it was so clear that she could see the Milky Way. But now dawn has broken, and clouds have moved in.

Since she first set foot in her school's science lab as a high school student in Damascus, Syria, Shadia has wanted to understand things such as magnetism and gravity—the forces that power and move our solar system. Now she is a solar physicist at the University of Hawaii. And she travels the world chasing eclipses, hoping they will help her unlock the secrets of the sun.

Once every eighteen months or so, the moon's orbit causes it to pass directly between the sun and the Earth. When this happens, the moon covers the photosphere, or the bright circle of the sun. The sky becomes as dark as night, and a ghostly white halo appears. This is the corona, or the atmosphere that surrounds the sun. And an eclipse is one of the few times scientists can get a good look at it.

A year earlier, in 2015, Shadia braved subzero temperatures (and polar bears) to lead an eclipse expedition to the island of Svalbard in the Arctic Circle. Her observations there

Judd Johnson sets up instruments in Svalbard.

arrived on an actual desert island in search of answers.

And it's cloudy.

Studying solar eclipses can lead scientists to breakthrough discoveries about the sun. But it's risky research. Eclipse expeditions can be expensive and challenging, taking scientists to remote and inaccessible locations in far corners of the world. The clock is always ticking. They have to be ready to start the experiment at the precise moment the eclipse begins, and they only have a few minutes to make their observations. There are no do-overs if they make a mistake. And if it happens to rain, or a wandering cloud passes in front of the sun at the wrong moment, the entire expedition will be a very expensive failure.

8

led to some surprising discoveries. She found strange disturbances in the corona, a turbulence that looked like smoke rings, that no one had seen before. She discovered that the way temperature is distributed around the corona was changing with the solar cycle, or the fluctuations in the sun's magnetic activity that increase and decrease every eleven years. Maybe most perplexing, she found cool material floating in a part of the corona that was very hot, where it was not supposed to be. What did it all mean? Shadia hoped her next eclipse would help her solve the mystery.

Now, a year later, after twenty-two hours in planes, five hours in cars, and ninety minutes bouncing across the water in speedboats, Shadia and her team of scientists and engineers have

The team in Svalbard.

As the day darkens into an eerie twilight, Shadia glances helplessly at her equipment, painstakingly calibrated and staring up at a sun that can't be seen. Through breaks in the clouds, she can see that the moon has nearly covered the solar disk. At precisely 9:53 a.m., the sky goes dark. Totality.

The small knot of tourists gathered on the beach cheers as they catch fleeting glimpses of the shimmering corona through the clouds. But Shadia can't enjoy the beautiful sight. Her heart sinks and she looks away, not wanting the rest of her team to see her deep disappointment. She might get some data from this eclipse, but not much. Certainly not enough to answer the questions that have been burning in her mind since Svalbard—and since she saw her first eclipse in India almost twenty years ago. This trip was almost a complete waste.

Now she'll have to wait a year and a half for another chance. Already, she's thinking ahead to her next eclipse, in North America in August of 2017. She has seventeen months to plan, and she'll need the time. This will be her biggest and most ambitious expedition yet.

9

Clouds blocked the team's view of the eclipse on Plun Island, Indonesia, on March 9, 2016.

The team on Plun Island.

CHAPTER 1
America's Eclipse

TWO MINUTES AND THREE SECONDS. That's how long Shadia would get to study what people were calling the Great American Eclipse.

On August 21, 2017, a total eclipse of the sun would cut across the United States from coast to coast for the first time in ninety-nine years. Every eclipse is remarkable, but what would make this one special was how many people would be able to see it. Even though total eclipses occur fairly often—about seventy-five times each century—much of the time, the moon's shadow passes over remote or unpopulated areas where no one is around to see it. An eclipse might pass over a desert, or across the open ocean. But this one would cross thirteen states, from Oregon to South Carolina. Some twelve million people lived directly in its path. Half of the country was within a day's drive. "For so many people to be so close to the path of totality is very rare," Shadia says. It was possible more people would see this eclipse than any other in history.

People traveled from all over the country—and around the world—to see the Great American Eclipse of 2017.

PATH OF TOTALITY

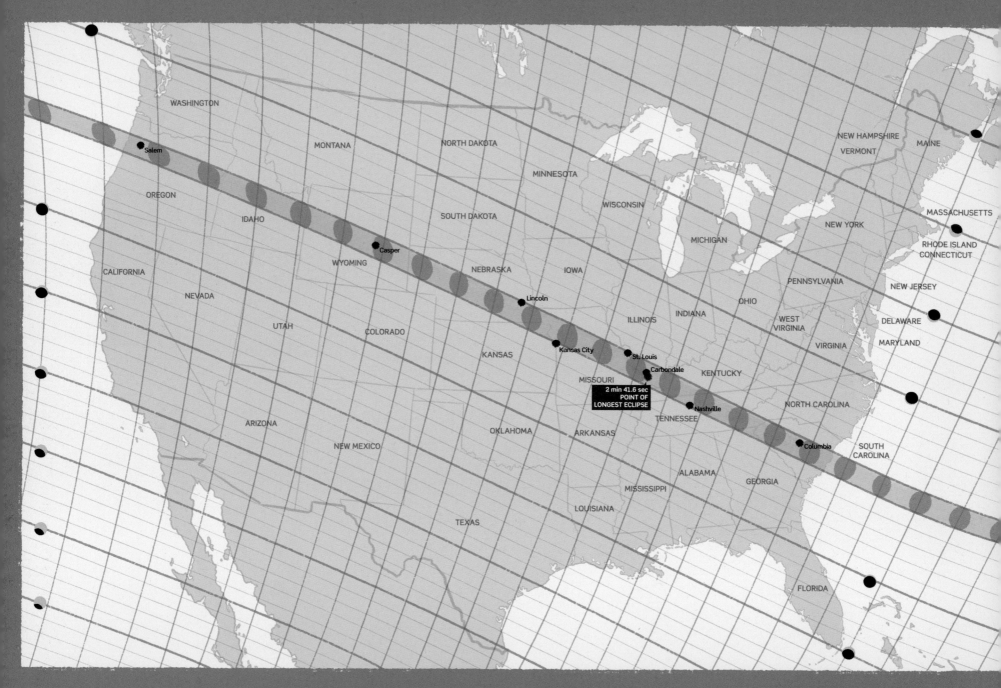

The path of totality for the Great American Eclipse cut across thirteen states.
The last time a total solar eclipse crossed the United States was ninety-nine years earlier.

For six years, Shadia had been helping the country get ready. She and other scientists and educators met with local governments, police and fire departments, state and national parks, private companies, and schools. They wanted people to be excited about the eclipse, but also prepared. They knew that millions of people would travel to see it. Many of them would want to be in rural areas and small towns. If these communities didn't plan ahead, they might be overwhelmed by tourists. They would need to find space for extra campgrounds, plan for traffic jams, and rent lots of portable toilets!

Shadia also talked to people about how to watch the eclipse. She wanted people to know how to protect their eyes and enjoy the eclipse safely, but she also wanted them to really see it. The partial phase of an eclipse can hurt your eyes if you look at it directly, but it's safe to look at the sun during totality—in fact, that's the only way to see it. "My concern is that people won't remove their glasses during totality," Shadia says. "I tell them, if you can't see anything anymore through the glasses, then you should remove the glasses and look at the corona."

Shadia was eager for people to see the corona; she thinks it's one of the most beautiful and amazing sights in nature. She also hoped that watching the eclipse would get more people interested in science. An eclipse is a chance for people to observe the actual movement of the

On a normal day, the sun is so bright that its corona, or atmosphere, fades into the background. But during a total solar eclipse, you can see the corona with your own eyes.

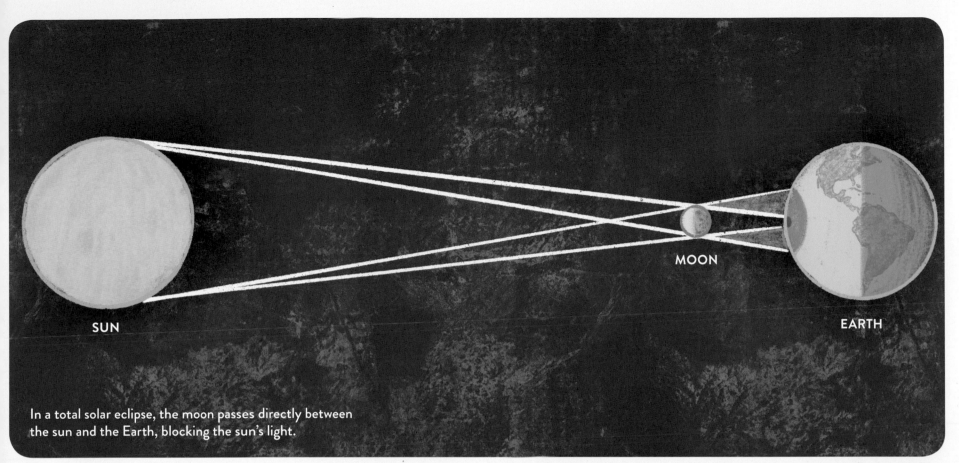

In a total solar eclipse, the moon passes directly between the sun and the Earth, blocking the sun's light.

SUN

MOON

EARTH

solar system, and to think about the forces that cause that movement, like gravity.

An eclipse is also a chance for people to see the sun in a new way, and learn about how it works and how it affects our planet. Many people may not even realize that stars have an atmosphere, but during an eclipse they can see the sun's atmosphere with their own eyes. What is that atmosphere made of? What gives it its shape and structure? What happens to that atmosphere as it streams out into space? As a scientist, Shadia felt a responsibility to share what she had learned with other people. As she

traveled around the country, she gave talks at schools and universities about her work and spoke to many journalists about the upcoming eclipse.

Shadia had loved science since she was a girl. The oldest of four sisters, she was born in Damascus, Syria. Syria has been devastated by a civil war that began in 2011. But when Shadia was growing up, it was a peaceful, progressive country, where education was valued. Her parents, both teachers, sent her to a missionary school, where she learned French and English, in addition to the Arabic she spoke at home.

It was her science teacher, Sister Bernard-Dominique, who introduced her to physics. Shadia liked how Sister Bernard-Dominique would come up with amusing stories and problems to solve, like asking her to calculate how much someone would weigh on the moon. For Shadia, it was like a light had turned on inside of her. A force like gravity did more than make your pencil fall off your desk. It moved planets, stars, and whole galaxies. By understanding the rules of physics, Shadia realized, you could understand how the whole universe worked.

Shadia's hero was Marie Curie, who conducted pioneering research on radioactivity through her experiments. "I found her life story fascinating," Shadia says. "She had the drive and the smarts and the imagination to carry out her experiments and make all these discoveries, and she also had to fight prejudices."

Her parents thought she might become a doctor, but Shadia had other plans. She wanted to become a physicist. She graduated from the University of Damascus, went on to study at the American University in Beirut, Lebanon, and then came to the United States to get her PhD in physics.

Now Shadia hoped this eclipse might inspire a new generation of physicists and astronomers. But she couldn't spend all her time talking about it. She had her own expedition to plan. And because this eclipse was so close to home, she wanted to put together a big team and bring as many telescopes, cameras, and observing instruments as she could. In the end, she was able to get

Shadia Habbal, a solar physicist with the University of Hawaii, leads a team of eclipse chasers called the Solar Wind Sherpas.

Shadia's team uses solar eclipses to learn about the sun's atmosphere, or corona.

more than twenty-five scientists and engineers from a dozen universities, observatories, private companies, and other institutions to help her make her observations. She spread them out at several different sites dotted along a one-thousand-mile (1,600 km) stretch of the eclipse's path.

Spreading out her team would increase the likelihood that at least some of her sites would have good weather. It would also mean that she could observe the corona over time. "You can follow dynamic changes in the corona when you're spread out," Shadia says. "At each site it's only two minutes and a few seconds, but if you put the pictures together from five or six sites, you can say, 'Look, the features changed from this to this to this.'"

Shadia began researching locations, contacting local chambers of commerce and community groups for help and advice. A year before the eclipse, she flew to meet

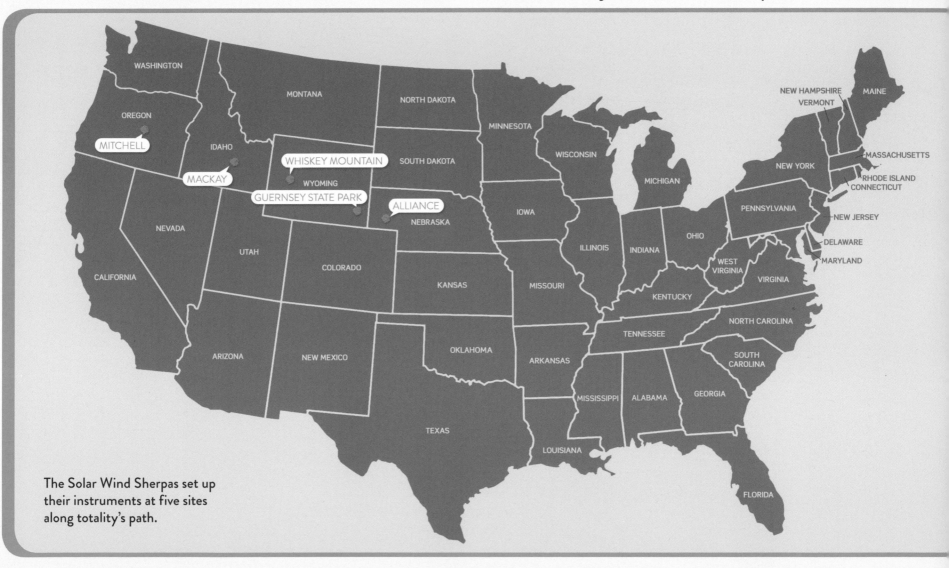

The Solar Wind Sherpas set up their instruments at five sites along totality's path.

18

Judd Johnson, an engineer in Boulder, Colorado, one of her closest and longest collaborators, for a scouting trip. Together they drove west from Nebraska, stopping to check out sites along the way. They were looking for places far away from city lights, with a dry climate and a clear view of the sky. The sites also had to be able to accommodate her team with housing, water, and electricity.

In the end, they found five sites that seemed perfect: Mitchell, Oregon; Mackay, Idaho; Whiskey Mountain and Guernsey State Park in Wyoming; and Alliance, Nebraska. Shadia started making the arrangements, but she kept her plans private—she didn't want any competing eclipse teams showing up at her designated spot.

Organizing such a big expedition was stressful. Besides planning her own scientific research and applying for funding, Shadia had to think about things like providing food, transportation, and housing for all those people. She had to assign groups, pick team leaders, and make sure everybody could work well together and get along.

Teamwork is essential when working on an eclipse. "There is a critical time issue," Shadia says. "It requires discipline on the part of everyone. If someone decides they want to do something their own way, it doesn't work. We all have to be ready and work together at the same time."

Fortunately, Shadia already had a team she could count on. She calls them the "Solar Wind Sherpas." That's because, like the Sherpa people of Nepal, who are famous for carrying heavy loads on long mountain treks, this group lugs their heavy telescopes and scientific equipment around the world. These scientists and engineers have chased eclipses with Shadia from the South Pacific to the Arctic Circle, and from Mongolia to the Middle East. They've shivered through blizzards together, gotten lost together, and eaten strange foods together. They've been with Shadia for her bitterest failures and her most exciting discoveries.

She knew they wouldn't let her down now.

Members of the 2017 eclipse expedition met up in Boulder, Colorado, before splitting up and traveling to five observing sites across the country.

SAFETY FIRST

Follow these tips to watch an eclipse safely:

- *Never look directly at the sun's surface. Even during a partial eclipse, when the sun might appear dimmer than normal, it can cause permanent damage to your eyes.*

- *You can watch a partial eclipse through eclipse glasses or solar viewers, which have special filters that block harmful light. Regular sunglasses won't protect your eyes.*

20

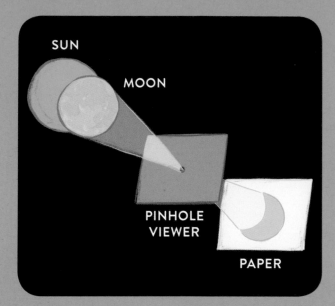

SUN

MOON

PINHOLE VIEWER

PAPER

- *Another way to see a partial eclipse is with a pinhole viewer. Make a tiny hole in a piece of cardboard and hold it above a smooth surface, like paper. As the sun shines through the pinhole, an image of the eclipse will appear on the paper below. You can also use objects with small holes, like colanders, to project the sun.*

- *During totality, when the surface of the sun is completely covered, look up! The solar corona is about as bright as moonlight, so it's safe to look at with your eyes—and you can't see it through eclipse glasses. Don't miss this spectacular sight!*

- *As soon as the sun begins to reappear, protect your eyes again.*

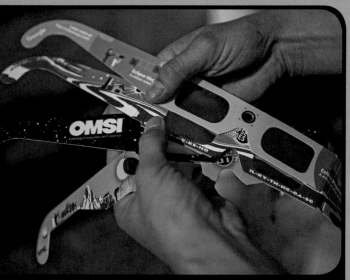

Eclipse glasses protect your eyes when looking at a partial solar eclipse.

THROWING SHADE

Any time the moon and the sun cross paths in the Earth's sky, it creates what scientists call an eclipse. But not all solar eclipses are the same.

- *A total eclipse occurs when the moon completely covers the sun. The sky goes dark, and you can see the pale corona.*

- *A partial eclipse occurs when the moon only moves partway in front of the sun. The sky might get a little darker, like on a cloudy day. You can watch the partially eclipsed sun by looking at it through a solar filter. During a total eclipse, if you're outside the path of totality, you might still be able to see the sun partially eclipsed.*

- *An annular eclipse occurs during periods when the moon's orbit takes it slightly farther away from Earth, making the moon appear smaller in the sky. The lunar disk isn't quite big enough to fully cover the sun, so it leaves a bright ring of fire in the sky.*

An annular eclipse.

The team traveled to the tiny town of Mitchell, Oregon, to observe the 2017 eclipse.

CHAPTER 2
Mitchell

"WATCH WHERE YOU STEP—there are rattlesnakes around here," warns the woman selling commemorative eclipse buttons, hats, and posters by the side of Highway 26, a few miles outside Mitchell, Oregon. Four hours east of Portland, Mitchell is a one-gas-station town that normally has a population of fewer than two hundred people. But today isn't normal. It's August 19, 2017. The town's park is filling up with tents, and the Little Pine Cafe has set up a big outdoor grill to cook hamburgers for all the tourists who are arriving to see the eclipse.

Mitchell is directly in the path of totality. Its desert climate also means it's likely to have good weather and clear skies on eclipse day. Those two factors are the reasons why so many eclipse chasers have come to this tiny town. They're also the reasons why Shadia is here.

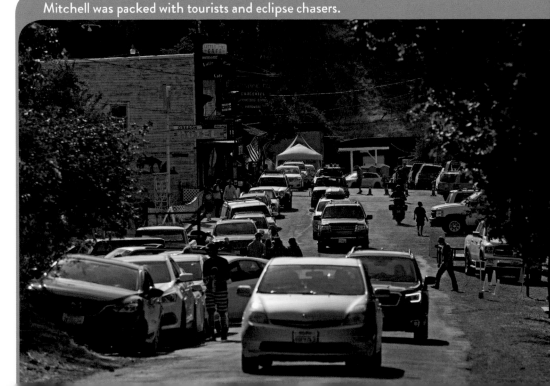
Mitchell was packed with tourists and eclipse chasers.

To get away from the crowds, Shadia made arrangements
to stay on a private ranch outside of town.

To avoid the crowds, Shadia has rented a farmhouse on a
working cattle ranch about forty minutes outside of town.
Most of her group caravanned in several days before, after
spending several days preparing and training with the rest of
the team in Boulder. It's a tight squeeze. They have filled up
all the beds and put air mattresses down on the floors. Those
who can't fit in the house are sleeping in the RV they rented
or have pitched tents in the yard.

These telescopes will take pictures of the corona in white light, or the kind of light people can see with the naked eye.

After settling in, they get to work, making sure their cameras, telescopes, and other equipment are ready to go. Even though the eclipse is still two days away, they have a lot to do. The instruments must be set up, aligned, calibrated, and checked. The computer systems that run the instruments must be connected and tested. Timers have to be linked, programmed, and checked. And the scientists must go over their plans, make test images, and practice what they will do during the eclipse.

The team sets up camp in the ranch house and yard.

A special tent protects the instruments from rain and dust. The roof can be opened up to make observations.

In some ways, it's easier now that computers run the observations. Shadia and her team used to have to operate their instruments manually. Now, they will simply click a button to start the program and step out of the tent a few seconds before the eclipse. There's no computer program you can buy that will run the kinds of experiments Shadia is doing, so Pavel Štarha, a mathematician from the Czech Republic, wrote a special one to do the job. Having Shadia's instruments computerized made many things easier, but it's also one more thing that needs to be set up, checked, and rechecked before the eclipse.

Judd Johnson is sawing through a piece of white plastic in his makeshift outdoor workshop. An engineer, Judd is often the one who helps Shadia figure out how to make her equipment do what she needs it to do. And when something goes wrong, he's often the person who figures out how to fix it.

Judd, an engineer, has collaborated with Shadia on all of her eclipse expeditions.

Pavel and Judd prepare a "flat field" to calibrate the telescopes. A flat field is used to check for irregularities in the lenses and sensors.

All things considered, preparations have gone smoothly in Mitchell so far, he says. Especially compared to some of their past trips. In Svalbard, for example, the base of an instrument mount got lost in transit. Judd searched the tiny, snowy island north of Norway until he found a heavy-equipment mechanic, who was able to quickly jerry-rig a replacement in his machine shop.

So far, the only problem in Mitchell is that the "flat field" they brought isn't quite the right size to fit the telescopes. This is a smooth tile of white plastic that is used to calibrate telescopes. Taking a picture of a flat field can show scientists if there are irregularities in their lenses or sensors. Now Judd is taking a larger piece of the material and cutting it down to the right size.

Shadia is using many different telescopes and cameras to make observations. Each gives her a different kind of

It takes several days to set up, align, calibrate, test, and practice with all the instruments before the eclipse.

Clouds make a beautiful sunset,
but are bad news for the eclipse.

Now Riad and Rafif have prepared a family-style dinner for everyone, and the team squeezes in around the kitchen table. As they fill their plates with chicken, potatoes, salad, and cookies, talk turns to past eclipses.

"My favorite one was Libya," Shadia says. "The place, the country . . ."

"The food?" asks Enrico Landi, a solar physicist from the University of Michigan.

"The food, not so much," Shadia laughs. "But we got great data. It was a turning point."

The kitchen falls quiet. With more telescopes looking at the sun than they've ever had before, Shadia and her team might make their next scientific breakthrough with this upcoming eclipse, just two days away.

If the weather is good.

"Shadia, on the twenty-first, will it be clear?" Rafif finally asks.

"The predictions change every hour," Shadia says with a small smile. "I hope it will be clear."

Shadia and Judd talk eclipses at the dinner table.

Sometimes a solar flare or storm on the sun is so strong that it causes a powerful explosion of magnetism and electrically charged particles to burst out of the corona and into space. Scientists call these eruptions coronal mass ejections, or CMEs.

Even though the sun is almost ninety-three million miles (150 million km) away, CMEs can affect life on Earth. That's especially true now that humans are so dependent on technology. When one of these bursts hits our planet, it can cause a geomagnetic storm that fries electrical equipment. These phenomena can disable satellites, damage computers, and even disrupt air travel. In 1989, a CME knocked out the entire power grid for the Canadian province of Quebec.

The most powerful coronal mass ejection ever recorded happened in 1859. On September 1, astronomers observed a solar flare so intense that it could be seen with the naked eye. A day later, Earth was hit by a massive burst of plasma, or positively and negatively charged particles from the sun. As the wave of energy splattered against our planet's magnetic field, it created auroras that were seen as far south as Cuba and Hawaii.

Energy traveled through the ground and up into human-made objects, like telegraph wires (before phones came along, telegraphs were a way of sending messages across long distances using electrical signals). The wires showered sparks, and telegraph operators reported feeling shocks.

Today, scientists hope that by learning more about the sun and how it works, they can better understand solar weather. Learning how to predict solar storms could someday help us to prevent millions of dollars in damage, protect the technology we depend on in our daily lives, and even keep astronauts safe from radiation in space.

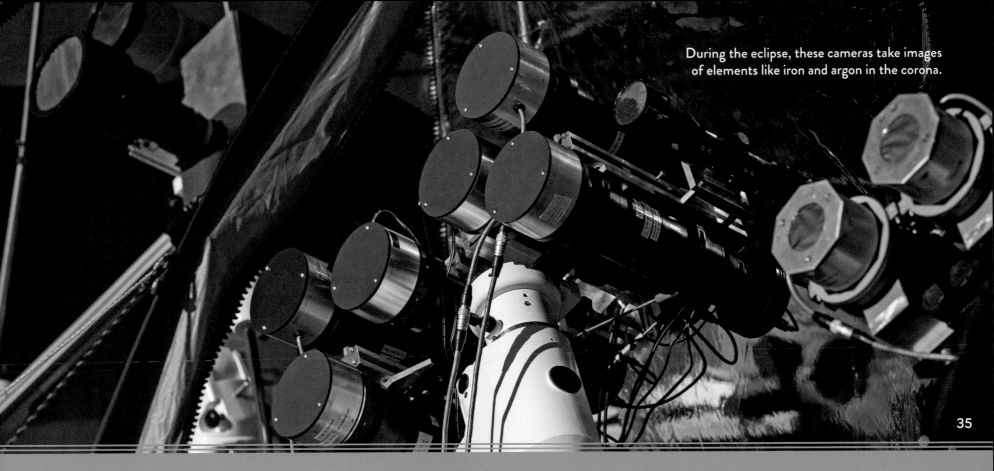

During the eclipse, these cameras take images of elements like iron and argon in the corona.

AN ECLIPSE CHASER'S TOOLS

Light is made up of energy moving in waves. These waves might be longer or shorter depending on the chemical elements that reflect the light. Each element reflects light at a unique wavelength. By using special instruments to observe light coming from the corona during an eclipse, Shadia and her team can learn things about the sun's atmosphere.

They use uses three main types of instruments:

- *Imagers. These powerful cameras are outfitted with special filters that block all light except the wavelength Shadia is looking for—the wavelength reflected by a single chemical element. By taking a picture of the eclipse with one of her filters, Shadia and her team can create an image that shows how this element is distributed around the corona.*

- *Telescopes and cameras. These take pictures in white light, without any filters. The pictures show the eclipse as it would appear to a human eye.*

- *Spectrometers. These instruments take a sample of light and break it up into the full spectrum of wavelengths it is made of, like a rainbow. Analyzing these wavelengths can tell scientists information about the kinds of particles that emitted the light.*

CHAPTER 3
Breakthrough

MARCH 29, 2006. LIBYA. The still-rising sun had thinned to a sliver in the cloudless sky. It wouldn't be long now.

Shadia carefully looked away from the sun before removing her eclipse glasses. When she had explored this area a year earlier to scout locations for her expedition, the Libyan Desert had struck her as vast, silent, and beautifully desolate, empty of people, except for the occasional band of nomads. She found the perfect spot, with a clear view of the sky overhead, and pebbles underfoot—not sand or dust, which could be kicked up by a gust of wind and ruin her observations. Now, Shadia found herself surrounded by a small tent city, complete with electricity, air conditioning, running water, and internet access, all courtesy of the Libyan military.

Even though the roads and facilities around her were spare, the people of Libya had been kind and welcoming to Shadia and her team. It didn't hurt that Shadia spoke fluent Arabic and knew the customs of the region. As much as she was excited by science and the thrill of discovery, Shadia also loved the adventure of her eclipse expeditions, traveling around the world and feeling welcomed by many different people. "I think there's something very touching about going to different places and experiencing the humanity of different cultures," she says.

Libya's government had gone overboard to provide facilities for the scientific teams and adventurous tourists who were here to view the total solar eclipse. Compared to some of her past eclipses, the setup was positively luxurious.

The Libyan government provided military planes to help the scientists transport their equipment to the desert.

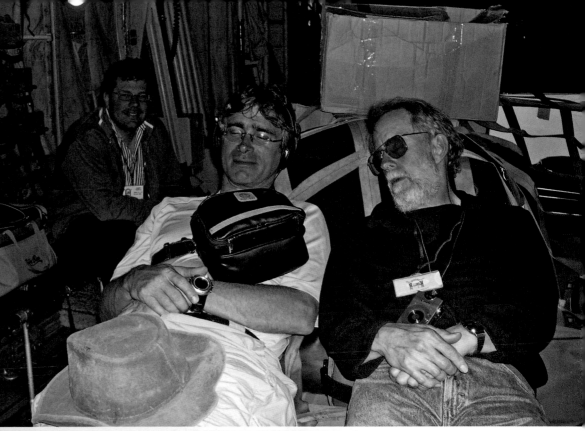

The team flew to a remote location in the Libyan Desert to view the eclipse.

The team sets up their tents and equipment in the Libyan Desert.

In addition to the comfortable accommodations, Shadia really could not have asked for better viewing conditions, she thought to herself as the light grew steadily dimmer. Three days earlier, a sandstorm had sent her team running to protect their equipment. But today, the weather was perfect, without a cloud in the sky. And with more than three minutes of totality, she hoped she had enough time to make her observations.

Shadia wanted to study the chemical elements in the corona. To do this, she would look for light reflected by atoms in the sun's atmosphere. Each atom reflected light in a specific color, or wavelength. "Each color corresponds to a different element," or an altered form of that element, she says. By filtering out all wavelengths except the one she was looking for, Shadia could make a picture that showed where that element was found in the corona.

Iron was one of the elements she had been studying. Iron is the most abundant element in the corona, and the way it reflects light also makes it very easy to see. But the main reason Shadia was interested in iron was because it's a useful tool for measuring the corona's temperature. That's because iron atoms change their form when they get very hot. (Other elements also do this, but these altered forms of iron are easy to see.) At a million degrees Celsius (1.8 million degrees F), some of iron's electrons fly off, breaking apart at the atomic level. Scientists call this altered form of iron *iron X* and *iron XI*. When the atoms get even hotter, approaching two million degrees Celsius

(3.6 million degrees F), more electrons break away. This creates *iron XIV*.

Many scientists have observed iron XIV in the corona. Shadia had studied it too, with good results. She'd also taken pictures of iron X. The pictures were fainter, but they were still intriguing. But nobody had ever made an image of iron XI in the corona, and Shadia wanted to try. She wasn't even sure it would be visible; its wavelength was right at the limit of what her equipment could detect. She'd hoped to get some images of iron XI at her last two eclipses, but she'd been clouded out both times. Now in Libya she would have another chance.

The trouble was, these eclipse expeditions were expensive. She could afford only a couple of imagers, special cameras with filters that block all light except the wavelength she was looking for. What if she dedicated one to look for iron XI, and it didn't work? She couldn't afford to take that risk. So Shadia came up with a plan to sneak a peek. She would use her imager to photograph iron XIV as planned. But a few seconds before the end of the eclipse, she'd quickly swap out the filter for iron XI. If all went well, she'd get a couple of images—enough to find out if iron XI was as interesting as she suspected.

A sudden twilight fell over the camp as the moon's shadow rushed across the desert. With less than a minute to go before totality, Shadia's team quickly and carefully slipped the covers off their instruments and took their places. Then the desert was plunged into darkness.

Totality above Libya.

Click. Click. Click. The scientists worked quickly and precisely, hunching together over the computers that controlled their cameras and telescopes. Using a stopwatch to keep track of time, they triggered exposure after exposure, just the way they had practiced.

Click. Click. Click. The seconds and minutes were ticking away. Everything seemed to be going according to plan, and Shadia felt almost positive she'd gotten some good pictures of iron XIV. Now was her chance. With less than a minute to go, she gave the signal to Huw Morgan, a researcher

Judd and Shadia celebrate after totality.

The Libyan total solar eclipse of March 29, 2006, was a breakthrough for Shadia's research.

working on her team. Together they slipped off the filter for iron XIV and replaced it with the one for iron XI, managing to snap a few images before the eclipse was over.

As the day brightened around them, Shadia and her team covered the lenses of their instruments once again, then broke out in smiles and cheers. She felt relieved, hopeful, and excited. The operation had gone nearly perfectly. She was sure she'd gotten more great pictures of iron XIV. But what about iron XI? She'd managed to make a few exposures with her telescope. When she looked at them, what would she see?

Shadia had been acting on a hunch, and it paid off. When she got back home and looked at her images, the pictures of iron XI were bright and clear. And what they showed her was surprising. Iron XI extended far out into the corona, and made many detailed shapes and structures in the sun's atmosphere. Shadia realized that while iron X showed her parts of the sun that were one million degrees Celsius (1.8 million degrees F), iron XI, which was nearly the same temperature, was a much better marker to see these cooler features of the corona.

Now, by comparing her observations of iron XI and iron XIV, Shadia could start to compare the temperatures in the corona. Putting them together would create a map of the corona that showed where it was hotter and where it was cooler. They had never been able to do this so clearly before.

41

This photograph from the total solar eclipse in Libya shows iron XI in the corona (in red).

Shadia and her colleagues made other discoveries from iron XI as well. They could see particles accumulating and clumping together in fine lines. These particles were being attracted to the sun's magnetic field lines, she realized. Magnetism is a powerful force that gives shape and structure to the corona, but it's invisible. Shadia uses the iron particles as tracers, allowing her to see the lines of magnetism.

They also identified, for the first time, the distance from the sun where particles stop gaining and losing electrons and their identities become fixed.

Shadia knew this was the beginning of a new chapter for her. More than a decade earlier, in India, she had begun to imagine what she could learn from eclipses. For the next ten years she had developed her methods by trial and error, often learning as much from her failures as she did from her successes. Now, as she studied her team's pictures from Libya, it seemed like all that work was starting to pay off. They weren't just chasing eclipses anymore—they were getting results. And Shadia was hungry for more.

THE SOLAR WIND

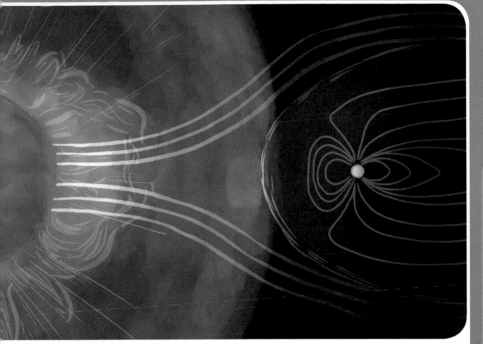

Earth's magnetic field protects it from the solar wind, a stream of protons, electrons, and atoms flowing out from the sun.

Thanks to the incredible heat of the corona, a steady stream of protons, electrons, and a few atoms gathers enough energy to escape the gravity of the sun and blow out into the solar system. This flow of particles is called the solar wind.

Just like a powerful breeze on Earth can knock the hat off your head, or even wear down mountains over time, the solar wind packs a lot of oomph. It's the reason a comet's tail always points away from the sun, blown outward by the solar wind, and it causes the auroras people sometimes see at the Earth's poles. It even blasts the atmosphere off planets like Mars—planets that don't have a strong magnetosphere, or a protective bubble of magnetism. And someday, spacecraft could use sails to ride the solar wind to distant planets.

But although scientists know the solar wind starts in the corona, they still don't understand what drives it, why some parts of it are fast and others slow, why it changes, and many other things about it. That's something Shadia hopes her work with eclipses will help her figure out.

WHY IS THE CORONA HOT?

If you hold your hand very close to the surface of a hot stove, you might get burned. But move your hand away from the stove, and the air cools down the farther away it gets. Makes sense, right? Not on the sun.

"The big mystery, which is still ongoing, is: What makes the corona so hot? People have been exploring this question for a long, long time," Shadia says. The center of the sun is thought to be an inferno of fifteen million degrees Celsius (27 million degrees F). By the time you get up to the sun's surface, things have cooled down a lot, to a balmy six thousand degrees Celsius (10,800 degrees F). But move up into the atmosphere, and instead of getting cooler, it gets hotter again—much hotter. The temperature of the corona eventually rises to as much as two million degrees Celsius (3.6 million degrees F).

Where does all that heat come from? How does it move from the surface of the sun up into the atmosphere? And does this strange temperature change have something to do with the solar wind? Shadia hopes that her observations of the corona during eclipses will give her new clues to solve the mystery.

The sun rises on the morning of the eclipse.

CHAPTER 4
Countdown

I'S A LITTLE AFTER SIX A.M. on August 21, 2017—eclipse day. Miloslav Druckmüller and Peter Aniol are standing on the back porch of the Mitchell farmhouse, looking up at the sky. The chilly morning air smells of freshly cut hay, and the rolling hills are lit up in golden light as the sun rises brilliantly in the east. But a thin, dirty-looking haze is smeared across the western horizon, and Peter doesn't like the look of it.

"This is deadly," he says, gazing at the sky.

Milos and Pavel check the sky. There's smoke on the horizon from wildfires burning to the west.

"It's crystal clear from the point of view of the weather," observes Miloslav. "This is smoke."

"Start the bagel production line." Shadia is standing at the sink, filling a carafe of water for a big pot of coffee. She looks calm as she moves around the kitchen, setting out plates, cups, fruit, and cream cheese with some young helpers. But on the inside, Shadia

Even these thin clouds could ruin Shadia's observations.

feels stressed to the limit. She has so many issues on her mind, she can't seem to focus. It's a good thing she's not responsible for operating any of the instruments today, she thinks to herself. That would be too much.

Then there's the smoke. Shadia has already been outside to look at it. For more than a week, wildfires have been raging in the western part of Oregon, burning thousands of acres of forest. The fires are hundreds of miles away, but they're big enough to stain the sky an ugly reddish brown. For now, it looks like the smoke is staying in the western part of the sky, but what if the wind blows it in their direction? There are also some thin, wispy clouds that are making Shadia nervous. It's not enough for the eclipse to simply be visible. The sky must be completely clear. If there are any particles of carbon or water vapor in the atmosphere, it could change how her observations turn out. But there's nothing Shadia can do about it now except hope for the best and make coffee.

Peter gets his telescopes ready.

Miloslav pulls an office chair up to the kitchen counter and opens his laptop. Milos is a mathematician from the Czech Republic. He helped Shadia plan the exposure times and sequences that would get her the best data. After the eclipse, he will spend months digitally processing Shadia's images. (It took him fifteen years to develop the sixty thousand lines of computer code he uses for this work.) But right now, he wants to check timing.

Milos and Enrico Landi double-check the timing of the eclipse.

Shadia helps Judd and Pavel check the imagers one last time.

Eclipse maps have predicted that C2, or second contact, the time at which the moon fully covers the sun, will begin at 10:20:53 a.m. But these calculations are based on the assumption that the moon is a circle. In reality, it's not. The lunar edge is actually jagged, with mountains and valleys. Milos checks a more precise calculation, one that takes into account the moon's actual shape. This one says second contact will actually begin 1.8 seconds earlier. Milos will adjust his timers accordingly.

While the rest of the team gets their instruments ready, Enrico Landi is also on his laptop. He is checking data on solar activity from observatories around the world and in space. It's like getting a weather report for the sun. He wants to know, *What's the sun doing today?*

49

Solar filters protect the cameras and telescopes from the damaging light of the sun. The scientists will remove the filters in the final seconds before totality begins.

Enrico is a solar physicist from the University of Michigan, and he doesn't usually work out in the field, making observations of the sun. In fact, this is his first eclipse. Enrico collaborates with Shadia by helping her study the data she gathers. Together, they brainstorm about what it might mean. When she is planning for an eclipse, he is one of the scientists she will talk to about what elements she will look for in the corona.

On this eclipse, she has chosen iron XIV, iron XI, nickel, and the gas argon. From spectroscopy, scientists know that argon exists in the solar atmosphere, but they've never imaged it before. Enrico is excited to try. "We hope to measure this in the solar corona, and that would be an absolute first," he says.

As a solar physicist, Enrico wants to understand how material on the surface of the sun gets up into the corona, and how it moves from there out into space and throughout the solar system on the solar wind. He and Shadia have a lot of questions. What types of particles are cast out from the sun? What causes them to move? How fast do they go? How are they changed by the sun's temperature and radiation? And where do they end up?

Scientists have studied eclipses for hundreds of years, but Shadia has found new ways to learn from them, Enrico says. Some see eclipses as too risky to study, because of the chance that bad weather might ruin everything. But by taking the risk and following her curiosity, Shadia has been able to try new things and make new discoveries

Solar physicist Enrico Landi collaborates with Shadia to study the data she gathers about the corona. He's excited to help make the first-ever observations of the element argon in the sun's atmosphere.

about the sun. "[Eclipses are] still probably the most underutilized technique in the field," Enrico says. "You never know whether you're going to get results or not, but if you do, it's breakthrough science."

A few minutes after nine a.m., Shadia is pacing restlessly by her instruments in the yard. "Do you have first contact?" she calls to Milos. He checks his watch. "In one minute, I think," he says.

The scientists get quiet as they huddle around their monitors, staring at the image of the sun, a perfect white circle against a field of black on the screen. For a moment, nothing happens. And then, the circle isn't quite so perfect anymore. The thinnest of slivers has been nibbled off one edge.

The eclipse has begun.

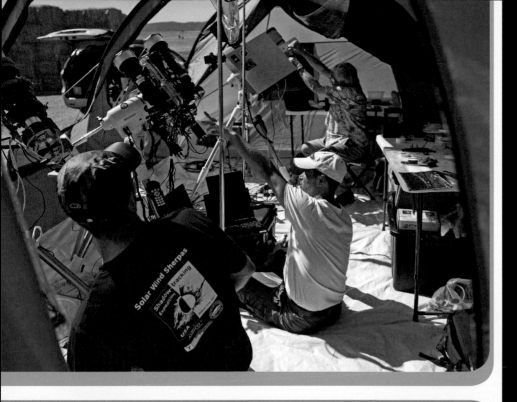

Enrico usually works with data, but not out in the field.
In fact, this is his first total solar eclipse!

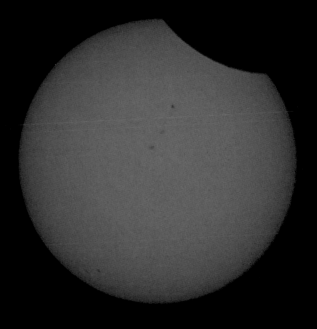

The moon takes a small bite out of the sun

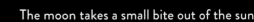

EYES ON THE SUN

There are many observatories on Earth and in space that study the sun. Some of them use a tool called a coronagraph to cover the solar disk, creating a kind of artificial eclipse so scientists can look at the corona anytime.

These observatories are powerful, but they also have limitations. Right now, none of them have cameras or telescopes that look at the elements Shadia wants to study in the corona. And getting a new instrument approved and added to one of these telescopes is extremely difficult and expensive.

By taking her own smaller, portable telescopes to eclipses, Shadia can decide for herself what she wants to observe. She can take a risk and try an observation or an experiment even if she's not sure it will get results. Some of those risks have paid off with important discoveries. Today, bigger observatories are building instruments to take a closer look at phenomena Shadia first observed on eclipses.

"Once you put a telescope in space, you're stuck with it," she says. "But with an eclipse, every time you can try something new."

MAPPING THE ECLIPSE

People traveling to the 2017 eclipse looked at maps to find out where they could go to see it. But how do scientists figure out the exact path of totality?

"It's actually pretty complicated," says eclipse mapper Michael Zeiler. Astronomers use precise measurements about the past movements of the sun, moon, and Earth to predict the course of their future orbits. Michael enters that data into a computer algorithm, or formula, to calculate where the moon's shadow will fall on Earth's surface during an eclipse. The calculation tells him the latitude and longitude of every point along the eclipse's path. It also tells him the exact time the partial eclipse will begin and end at every location, and the time that totality will begin and end.

In all, it takes about fifty million data points to create one of Michael's eclipse maps.

Astronomers have been using the same basic equations to determine the path of eclipses for more than 350 years. But thanks to computers and modern telescopes, today's eclipse maps are super precise. They can even take into account how a mountain or valley on the surface of the moon might change the start of totality ever so slightly.

"Now we have the technology to make it extremely accurate," says Michael.

This map shows the paths, dates, and durations of
solar eclipses occurring between 2011 and 2060.

A yellow line marks the path of a total solar eclipse.

An orange line marks the path of an annular eclipse.

A purple line shows the path of an eclipse that is total in some places
and annular in others, also known as a hybrid solar eclipse.

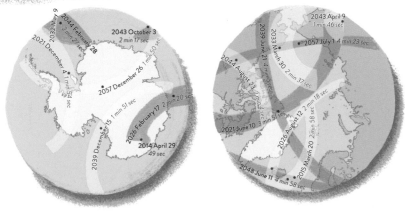

CHAPTER 5
Totality

"THERE ARE MANY THINGS THAT CAN GO WRONG," says Adalbert Ding. "Till now, we are lucky."

"Adi" is making a last check of his spectrometer. A physicist from Germany, he had been using spectrography to study chemical reactions in a laboratory when he met Shadia at a scientific conference. She invited him to join her team and apply his techniques to the solar corona. Adi was intrigued by the science and adventure of studying eclipses. "The processes I was looking at in the lab were also happening in space," he says.

Physicist Adalbert Ding has collaborated with Shadia on several eclipse expeditions.

Since his first eclipse with Shadia in 2009, Adi has seen firsthand how an eclipse can go wrong. In Kenya, it took days of bargaining with local officials to get their instruments released from customs. Then they had to drive two and a half days into the bush to the observing site and set up their equipment. "It was a perfectly clear sky, but then

Adi makes a last check of his spectrometer before the eclipse. This instrument will take a sample of light from the corona and split it into the spectrum of wavelengths it is made of. Analyzing these wavelengths gives scientists information about the particles that reflected the light.

The scientists monitor the progress of the eclipse as it approaches totality.

twenty minutes before the eclipse, a sandstorm came and covered everything," he says. "It was a total loss. And then we had to drive two and a half days back over those roads. The mood wasn't very cheerful."

56   Here in Mitchell, Shadia is feeling encouraged. "It's getting much better now," she says, gazing up at the sky. The smoke is staying out of the way, and the thin clouds that had worried her this morning seem to be breaking up. "It's dispersing."

If you watch the sun through a pair of eclipse glasses now, it looks like someone has taken a big bite out of a round cookie. There's no mistaking the dark silhouette of the moon, sliding slowly in front of the sun.

Look around the yard, and you'll see the scene on Earth is changing too. It's getting darker—not like the warm glow of a sunset, but as if someone is dimming the lights in a theater. Shadows take on a strange sharp quality. Under the trees, hundreds of little crescents appear in the dappled light; the tiny gaps between the leaves act as natural pinhole lenses.

"Ten minutes!" Judd calls. "Ten minutes to totality!"

The team takes their places. Now that computers run the cameras and telescopes, the scientists stay away from the instruments—they don't want to run the risk that someone will bump a camera or knock over a tripod in the dark. Judd and Pavel stand by to start the imagers, while Milos is responsible for starting the white-light cameras. When she sees everything is under control,

Shadia walks away, finding a place to stand by herself on the far side of the yard, her back to her instruments. She's too stressed out to be any closer.

The last few minutes before totality happen fast. The sun's crescent has thinned to a sliver. The final warm rays of daylight fade to an eerie gray. The swallows that had been zooming overhead disperse, retreating to their nests. The air cools—in some places the temperature can drop by as much as ten degrees Fahrenheit (6 degrees C) during an eclipse. Buzzing insects go silent. With less than sixty seconds to go, the scientists remove the solar filters, press Start, and then step away. It's safe to look at the eclipse without eclipse glasses now. For a few seconds, the sun is a thin white circle, sparkling with bright points of light. Then the false night falls, the sky turns a deep blue-black, and a ghostly white halo glows out of the darkness.

The corona is spectacular, reaching millions of miles out into space with long, soft white plumes—the classic angel-wings shape of the solar minimum, a period of low magnetic activity in the solar atmosphere. Shadia can see an angry red solar prominence jutting out from the surface of the sun along one edge. Just above the eclipse, the planet Venus hangs in the sky like a solitary blue diamond. "Wow!" she gasps.

For years, Shadia spent eclipses so focused on running her experiments that she sometimes forgot even to look at the sky. Now that computers run the program, she is finally free to watch the entire eclipse with her own eyes.

Shadia takes in a glorious totality.

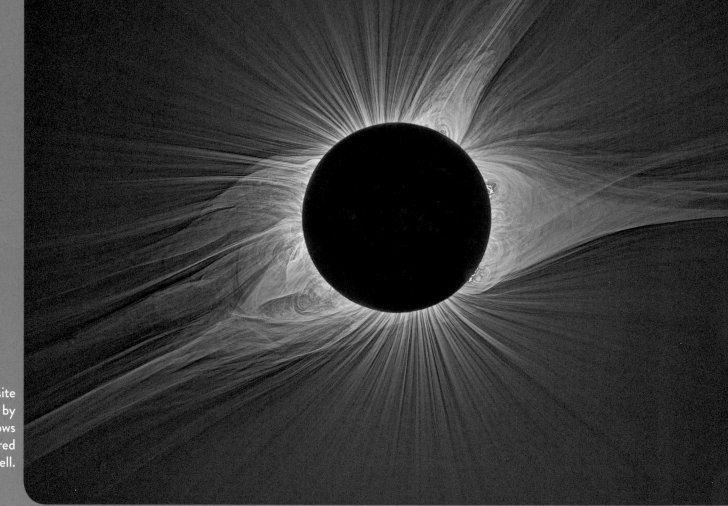

This image, a composite of photographs taken by several cameras, shows the corona as it appeared above Mitchell.

Click, click, click, click, click, click, click. The hush of the desert is interrupted by the soft *rat-a-tat* of Shadia's cameras firing, like paparazzi shooting a celebrity on the red carpet. But standing near the white-light telescopes, Milos can hear that something is not quite right. He was having problems with the timers yesterday. Now it sounds like one of the cameras is not working properly, but he can't tell which one. There's nothing he can do about it now, in any case. He puts it out of his mind and looks back up at the sky to enjoy the beautiful sight.

"Wow, wow, wow." No matter how many times he has seen it, Peter Aniol never gets tired of totality. Peter is the director of a telescope company in Germany, and he has brought a telescope to make white-light images. Like many of the Sherpas, Peter is not just a scientist, he's also an eclipse chaser. He has been to eighteen total solar eclipses. (Annular and partial eclipses he doesn't count.) But with the clear desert sky and spectacular corona, and surrounded by so many friends, this one feels special.

Time seems to stand still as the feathery silver plumes

of the corona dance and shimmer in the vast blue darkness. Then a moment later, the corona is pierced by a blinding white light. As the moon continues its slow slide across the sky, the sun's fiery face blazes forth once again. The scientists quickly move in to cover their lenses, protecting their instruments from the intense sunlight, and Shadia turns to face her team with a huge smile. "Fantastic!" She beams, as everyone breaks out in applause. "Gorgeous corona! You could see the streamers!"

The team cheers and hugs one another. Everyone is relieved—and excited to see if they got the data they were looking for.

Shadia celebrates after the eclipse. In spite of the clouds and smoke that had worried the team, the sky was clear during totality.

The scientists exchange hugs, smiles, and sighs of relief. Shadia quickly checks the imagers, and is happy to see that they all worked perfectly. The spectrometer did too.

Meanwhile, Milos takes a closer look at the white-light cameras. Just as he suspected, the timer on one of the seven cameras malfunctioned—it took just a single image during the eclipse. He's frustrated, but at least the other cameras took lots of pictures. Milos quickly checks his computer to take a peek at the images, and looks up with a grin. "Shadia!" he says, waving her over. "I've never seen prominences like this. The images are razor sharp. Unbelievable!"

Shadia smiles as she admires the pictures, then she gets on the phone. The eclipse may be over in Mitchell, but the shadow of the moon is still racing toward her other observing sites, and she wants to check in. "Mike? This is Shadia," she says, calling the team in Guernsey State Park, Wyoming. "Just to let you know, we got data. They weren't perfect-perfect, but they were very, very, very good. Okay? Good luck. I'll call you after your eclipse."

As the eclipse moves across the country, Shadia calls ahead to her team in Guernsey, Wyoming, to wish them good luck.

A quick check shows that the telescopes and imagers made great observations.

As her teammates crowd around to offer hugs and congratulations, Shadia's grin grows wider, the tension relaxing from her face. There's still work to do. First and foremost, she wants to save and back up her data. Then they'll begin the process of packing up their instruments and breaking camp. She'll want to check in with all her other sites as the day goes on. Once everyone is home, the team will spend the next year or more analyzing the data they've gathered. Hopefully, they will have new discoveries to share.

But all that will come later. Right now, Shadia just wants to enjoy this moment. The expedition was a success. After nearly two decades of chasing eclipses around the world together, this group of scientists and engineers has become more than colleagues. They are friends. And today, together, under a clear blue desert sky, it's time to celebrate.

The Mitchell team after totality.

THE SOLAR CYCLE

Every eclipse looks different. Sometimes the corona looks like a bunch of bright narrow spikes, and sometimes it is pale and feathery, reaching far out into space in fat, long plumes. That's because the sun's magnetism, which gives the corona its structure, ebbs and flows over the eleven-year solar cycle.

During the first part of the solar cycle, magnetic activity in the sun increases. Magnetic field lines get wound up so tight that they eventually snap. This stirs up the sun's atmosphere, causing lots of solar flares and coronal mass ejections. You can see this stormy weather in the sun's corona

This 2008 eclipse over Mongolia occurred near solar minimum. Magnetic activity has calmed down, and the corona fans out to either side in long, wispy streamers.

This eclipse over Australia in 2012 occurred near solar maximum, when the sun's atmosphere is very magnetically active, causing the corona to appear stormy and spiky.

during an eclipse, when lots of spiky streamers stick out in all directions, like a Mohawk. When the activity reaches a peak, this is called solar maximum.

Then things start to calm down. The sun's magnetic field lines relax. There are fewer solar flares, and the atmosphere becomes less turbulent. During an eclipse, you can see the corona swept smoothly outward from the sun's equator by the solar wind, like a graceful pair of wings. This is called solar minimum.

At the end of the eleven-year cycle (why it's always eleven years is still a mystery), the sun's magnetism flips, shifting from its north pole to its south, or vice versa. Then the pattern begins again.

Many people become eclipse chasers—not just scientists!

EPILOGUE

ECLIPSES HAVE ENTHRALLED HUMANS for thousands of years. Astronomers in ancient China and Babylon not only recorded solar and lunar eclipses, but learned how to predict them. Some civilizations created myths to explain eclipses, while others saw them as omens of terrible events. Scientists have been "chasing" eclipses for hundreds of years, sailing around the world to observe them.

Today, people chase eclipses for many reasons. Some are space and astronomy enthusiasts who geek out on seeing the sun's corona. For others, an eclipse is a spiritual experience. Many just want to see a spectacular sight and enjoy the adventure. For Shadia, it's not the beauty of eclipses, but what they can tell her about the sun, that keeps her coming back. "Some people are real addicts," she says. "I always wonder, if I stopped doing science, would I chase eclipses? And the answer is: I don't know."

It's a rainy March day in Honolulu when Shadia sinks into her chair at the

University of Hawaii Institute for Astronomy. Six months after the Great American Eclipse, Shadia feels like she has only recently begun to unwind. In more than two decades of studying eclipses, her 2017 expedition was the biggest and most stressful she ever attempted.

But it seems like all that stress was worth it. Shadia got great results. Thanks to the near-perfect conditions and hard work, the team's observations of iron, argon, and nickel were detailed and very high quality. The spectroscopy results are still being processed, but it looks as if they got good observations there as well. She'll be studying this data for years to come.

Shadia is especially excited that the cameras and telescopes caught a coronal mass ejection during the eclipse. The images show how this eruption of plasma and magnetic fields bursts through the corona, leaving a trail of turbulence in its wake. Surprisingly, her team's observations show that the material shooting up from the sun's surface stayed relatively cool, and didn't lose electrons, even as it passed through the scorching-hot corona. That's about as surprising as watching an ice cube float in a bowl of soup without melting. "It keeps its identity. It doesn't change. The big question is, how does this happen?" Shadia asks. "It's at ten thousand degrees [Celsius; 18,000 degrees F], and the corona is a million [degrees Celsius; 1.8 million degrees F]. How does it not ionize?"

Shadia is inspired to study eclipses because of what they can teach her about the sun.

It's the same phenomenon she saw at Svalbard—something so strange, she thought it might be a fluke. Now she knows that it's not unusual at all. She's discovered another solar mystery to be solved.

And what about argon? Shadia succeeded in taking the first pictures ever made of argon in the corona. But the results were surprising. It was very faint. Is that because there's not much of it in the solar atmosphere? Or could it be that levels of the gas will increase later in the solar cycle? Shadia will have to observe it again in four or five years to find out.

With the data she collected in 2017, Shadia will add a few new pieces to the puzzle, giving her some exciting clues about the sun and how it works. But she's hungry for more. Already she's planning her next eclipse expedition, for the summer of 2019, to South America. With clear skies, and if nothing goes wrong, she could learn something that brings her one step closer to understanding the mysterious star at the center of our solar system.

"People always ask me, 'You're at the mercy of the weather—is it really worth all this effort and expense?'" Shadia says, "And I say, 'Yes.'"

The team's observations of iron XI (in red) and iron XIV (in green) in the solar corona during the 2017 eclipse provide new clues about what's happening in the sun's atmosphere.

Guernsey team leader Nathalia Alzate (right) works with Solar Wind Sherpas
Keith Wood (in hat) and Scott Gregoire to set up the instruments.

GUERNSEY, WYOMING

When Shadia needed someone to lead her team in Guernsey, Wyoming, she chose Nathalia Alzate. "Naty" is a solar physicist who had helped out on several of Shadia's past expeditions. But this was her first time being in charge, so she was nervous. Would the team listen to her? She knew Shadia couldn't afford to have one of her teams make a mistake because they couldn't get along.

It turned out the rest of her group was in the same boat. Some of them had been to eclipses before, but it was their first time being responsible for running the equipment. "We were all thinking the same thing: this is our first time—we want to do a good job!" she says. "Once we discovered that about each other, we worked really well together."

Naty's team had arranged to stay in Guernsey State Park. They set up their instruments in a tent and camped in a yurt nearby, on a grassy hill overlooking a lake. The scenic park attracted lots of tourists eager to see the eclipse, but officials had blocked off a separate area for the scientists. Much as Naty likes sharing her science with people, she was glad. "We were isolated, which was very important," she says. "You don't want people running around messing up the equipment." And flash photography could ruin their observations.

On the wall of the tent, the team had posted a sign: "11:47." That was the exact time the eclipse would begin. All morning, the team had a clock running, watching the hours and minutes count down to totality. Even as she checked the weather and monitored the equipment, Naty kept an eye on

The Guernsey team posted the eclipse times where everyone could see them.

the clock. "The last thing you want to worry about is missing the minute or the second when you're supposed to start the computer to run the telescopes," she says.

During totality, Naty gazed up at the sky, smiling to herself as she heard her teammates gasp in awe, or call out, "This is amazing!" For some, it was their first eclipse. But Naty was happy to watch in quiet contemplation.

"I'm a very emotional person," she says. "There's those few seconds of, *Oh my God, this is an incredible event in the universe. Just the thought of what's happening: three bodies in space aligning to give us this event. Those are the things I think about, and just how lucky I am to be able to witness it."

ALLIANCE, NEBRASKA

When Martina Arndt woke up on eclipse day, she saw what she had been dreading: fog. The Massachusetts astrophysicist was in charge of Shadia's Alliance, Nebraska, team. They had set up their equipment at the private home of a local family and spent the last several days prepping for the eclipse. "You couldn't see beyond their driveway. It was very thick," Martina says of the fog. "We sat there and panicked."

The fog was just the latest challenge faced by the Alliance team. When they were setting up, sunlight had leaked into one of their cameras, burning a sensor. After consulting with Shadia on the phone, they'd swapped the filter from the damaged camera with one that was making less important observations, so they could still get the data she most needed.

Then, the heavy instrument mount that was supporting their telescopes kept sinking into the soft ground and tilting to the side. With help from their host family and a handy tractor, they moved the two-hundred-pound setup to a concrete pad. "With that stable surface, things worked out much better," Martina says.

But they couldn't do anything about this fog. "The family came out and sat with us and had coffee, and they said, 'Don't worry about it, it'll burn off,'" she says. "And they were right!"

By the time the eclipse started, it was a bright, sunny day. Martina's team went into action. They got the instruments ready, made sure all their equipment was charged in case the power went out, and got their computers turned on and ready to go. "It was intense and focused; there wasn't much socializing," she says. Ten seconds before totality, they started the program. "Once we hit Start, all of us took our hands away, stepped back, and didn't move," she says. "For two minutes, everyone was just enjoying it."

As soon as the eclipse was over, the scientists covered their instruments to protect them from the sun. Then they cheered. What's the first thing Martina did after hugging and congratulating her colleagues? She backed up her data! "In case someone spills coffee on the computer, you always want to have duplicates," she says. "It's a small step that can save a lot of agony."

The team in Alliance, Nebraska, set up their telescopes in a local family's front yard.

Alliance team leader Martina Arndt prepares for the eclipse.

Tülin Bedel, a member of the Solar Wind Sherpas' team in Alliance, Nebraska, operates the white-light cameras.

GLOSSARY

annular eclipse—An eclipse that occurs when the moon is at a farther point from Earth in its orbit, making it appear smaller in the sky, so that a ring of the sun's photosphere remains visible.

atmosphere—The bubble of gases that surrounds a planet or the sun.

corona—The atmosphere of the sun.

74 coronagraph—An instrument that blocks light from the sun, so that a telescope can view the corona.

coronal mass ejection—A powerful burst of plasma and magnetism from the sun.

eclipse—When one object in space moves into the shadow of another.

element—A substance that is already in its simplest form, which cannot be broken down into other substances.

gravity—The force of attraction between objects with mass.

ionization—The process in which an atom loses or gains electrons.

magnetic field—The area surrounding a magnetic object, like a star or planet, where its magnetism is effective.

magnetism—The force that causes magnetic objects to attract or push away other objects.

photosphere—The bright surface of the sun.

solar cycle—The pattern of increasing and decreasing magnetic activity in the sun, which repeats every eleven years.

solar system—The collection of eight planets as well as moons, asteroids, and other objects that move around the sun.

solar wind—The flow of charged particles away from the sun and out through the solar system.

spectrometer—An instrument that splits light into its different wavelengths.

telescope—An instrument that gives a larger view of a distant object.

totality—The moment of an eclipse in which the moon's disk completely covers the sun.

75

wavelength of light—The unique wave pattern made by electromagnetic radiation as it moves across space as a beam of light. Every color of light has a different wavelength.

SELECTED SOURCES

Alzate, Nathalia. "2015 Blog—Svalbard." The Solar Wind Sherpas: Total Solar Eclipse Chasers in Search of the Physics of the Corona and the Solar Wind. Accessed October 16, 2018. project.ifa.hawaii.edu/solarwind sherpas/blog/2015-tse-svalbard.

———. "The Solar Wind Sherpas: A 2016 Indonesia Adventure." The Solar Wind Sherpas: Total Solar Eclipse Chasers in Search of the Physics of the Corona and the Solar Wind. Accessed October 16, 2018. project.ifa.hawaii.edu/solarwindsherpas/blog/2016-tse-indonesia-2.

Golub, Leon, and Jay M. Pasachoff. *Nearest Star: The Exciting Science of Our Sun*. New York: Cambridge University Press, 2014.

NASA. "Total Solar Eclipse: August 21, 2017." Accessed October 16, 2018. eclipse2017.nasa.gov.

Nordgren, Tyler. *Sun Moon Earth: The History of Solar Eclipses from Omens of Doom to Einstein and Exoplanets*. New York: Basic Books, 2016.

Zeiler, Michael. "Great American Eclipse." Accessed October 16, 2018. greatamericaneclipse.com.

PHOTO CREDITS

Page 6: Miloslav Druckmüller, Peter Aniol; pages 7, 8 (upper left), 9 (left), 51: Nathalia Alzate and the Solar Wind Sherpas; pages 8 (lower right), 9 (right), 19, 36, 37, 38, 41: Shadia Habbal; page 21: Mike Kentrianakis/American Astronomical Society; page 40: Miloslav Druckmüller, Peter Aniol, image processing by Miloslav Druckmüller; page 42: Shadia Habbal, Huw Morgan, Judd Johnson, Martina Arndt, image processing by Miloslav Druckmüller; page 60: Miloslav Druckmüller, Peter Aniol, Shadia Habbal, image processing by Miloslav Druckmüller; page 64: Miloslav Druckmüller, Peter Aniol, Martin Dietzel, Vojtech Rušin, image processing Miloslav Druckmüller; page 65: David Finlay, Constantinos Emmanoulidis, Miloslav Druckmüller, image processing by Miloslav Druckmüller; page 69: Miloslav Druckmüller, Shadia Habbal, Pavel Štarha, Judd Johnson, Jana Hoderová, image processing by Miloslav Druckmüller; page 70: K. Teramura and the Solar Wind Sherpas; page 71: Michael Nassir, University of Hawaii; pages 72 and 73: Robert Havasy.

Maps on pages 12 and 53: Michael Zeiler, GreatAmericanEclipse.com.

ACKNOWLEDGMENTS

This book would not have been possible without the help and support of the Solar Wind Sherpas, most especially their fearless leader, Shadia Habbal. From the start, Shadia was beyond generous with her time and knowledge, spending many hours patiently explaining the complex and fascinating science that is the focus of her research. Shadia allowed us to join her expedition, made space for us to pitch our tent alongside her team, answered our many questions in the field, and even invited us to sit down to dinner and enjoy a plate of her delicious roast chicken. Finally, Shadia provided invaluable help in reviewing this manuscript for scientific accuracy and sharing personal photographs from her past eclipse expeditions. Thank you, thank you, thank you!

We would also like to thank the other members of the Sherpas, and their many friends, who made us feel welcome in Mitchell. Judd Johnson, Peter Aniol, Adalbert Ding, Miloslav Druckmüller, Pavel Štarha, Enrico Landi, Carolyn Wendeln, Clara Lin, Alina Schmalt, Louise Ching, and Riad and Rafif Rifai were gracious in sharing with us not only their knowledge, insight, and stories, but also a very small bathroom.

We are grateful to Nathalia Alzate for providing many photographs from the Great American Eclipse and past expeditions, and for sharing her experience in Guernsey. Martina Arndt generously took time to speak about the eclipse in Alliance. Others who provided valuable information and background for this book include Michael Zeiler and Mike Kentrianakis.

Finally, we would like to send a big thank-you to Kelly Sonnack of Andrea Brown Literary Agency, as well as Scientists in the Field editors Cynthia Platt, who worked on this book through "first contact," and Erica Zappy Wainer, who saw it through to "totality."

INDEX

Note: Page references in **bold** indicate photographs.

78

SCIENTISTS IN THE FIELD
Where Science Meets Adventure

Check out these titles to meet more scientists who
are out in the field—and contributing every day to
our knowledge of the world around us:

Looking for even more adventure? Craving updates on the work of your favorite scientists, as well as
in-depth video footage, audio, photography, and more? Then visit the Scientists in the Field website!

sciencemeetsadventure.com